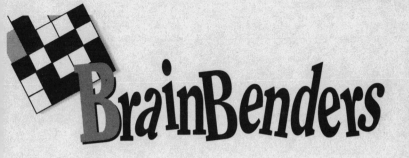

BrainBenders

by Dan Nevins

Watermill Press

Welcome!

In this exciting book, you'll find crossword puzzles, word finds, kriss-kross puzzles, missing-letter games, scrambled words, and much more. So grab a pencil and get ready for fun! If you get stumped, answers begin on page 42.

Starting with the letter G, count off each third letter. Go around the box three times, and be careful not to use the same letter more than once. You should be able to spell out the names of eight animals.

G R O I A W R B L A
A   B
Y   M
R   F
M   I
E   O
E   F
U   T
K   L
T   E
P   R
R S K U O L T O E E

Answers:

_____ _____ _____ _____

_____ _____ _____ _____

Circle the names of the following countries in the puzzle.
Look across, up and down, and diagonally.

CANADA   CHAD   CHINA   FRANCE
GERMANY   HUNGARY   IRAQ   IRELAND
ISRAEL   JAPAN   LAOS   MALI
PERU   POLAND   RUSSIA

```
F  R  A  N  C  E  H  I  Y
X  I  R  A  Q  W  U  S  C
I  G  J  A  P  A  N  R  A
R  U  S  S  I  A  G  A  N
E  C  G  A  Q  R  A  E  A
L  H  C  E  Z  Y  R  L  D
A  I  S  X  R  M  Y  N  A
N  N  L  D  A  M  A  S  Z
D  A  A  M  A  L  A  L  A
F  H  O  L  O  K  T  N  I
C  C  S  P  E  R  U  I  Y
```

Across

1. Arctic mammal with tusks.
6. Opposite of poor.
8. Oak-tree seed.
10. Opposite of cold: _ _ T.
11. Venus and Mars are _ _ _ _ E T S.
12. A wall that holds back water.
13. Opposite of him.
15. Pa's wife.
16. Walks with an injured leg.
18. Run (rhymes with hot).
20. Opposite of stop.
21. Opposite of in.
22. Small fairy-tale creature.
24. Small river.

Down

1. Moby Dick was this kind of animal.
2. Animal known as the "King of the Jungle."
3. Ancient vase (rhymes with turn).
4. Spanish for yes (rhymes with tea).
5. Tom's proper name.
7. Heavyweight _ _ _ _ _ of the world.
9. Rabbit's favorite food.
11. Snapshot.
14. Big striped cat.
17. Small animal that makes tunnels.
19. Move fast.
23. Fourth note of the musical scale.

Word Ladder • 7

As you go down a step in each puzzle, subtract one letter
to form a new word. Each step has a clue to help you.

1. **BLAME**
  2. _ _ _ _   Disabled or hurt.
   3. _ _ _   Baby sheep: _ _ _ B.
    4. _ _   Sixth note of the musical scale.
     5. _   First letter.

1. **PLANET**
  2. _ _ _ _ _ _   Flying machine.
   3. _ _ _ _ _   To _ _ _ _ _ a party.
    4. _ _ _ _   Fry bacon in this.
     5. _ _   Ma's husband.
      6. _   Sixteenth letter.

1. **FINGER**
  2. _ _ _ _ _ _   Nicer.
   3. _ _ _ _ _   Nice.
    4. _ _ _ _   A shark has one.
     5. _ _   Go _ _ to the room.
      6. _   Me.

8 • Missing Letters

All the words below contain the letters I and S.
Can you fill in the missing letters? Each word has a clue.

1. I S __ __ __ __   Land surrounded by water.

2. __ I S __   Animal that swims.

3. __ I S __   Workshop gripper.

4. __ __ __ I S   Place to find water in the desert.

5. __ I S __ __ __   Sibling.

6. __ I S __ I S __ __ __ __ __   Southern U.S. state.

7. __ I S __   Smooch.

8. __ __ __ __ I S __   Vow.

9. __ I S __   Moisture in the air.

10. __ I S __ __ __   Opposite of Mrs.

Do this puzzle like a regular crossword. But instead of filling in squares, put one letter in each triangle. For example, fill in the word FISH like this:

Across
1. The farmer grows a _ _ _ _ of wheat.
3. Finished.
5. Last word of a prayer.
6. Perspire.
7. Ice pellets from the sky.
8. Fairy-tale creature that lives under a bridge.
9. I don't have a _ _ _ _ (rhymes with dare) in the world!
11. Gorillas.
12. Mammal with flippers (rhymes with deal).

Down
1. Study very hard the night before a test (rhymes with tram).
2. Not closed.
3. Round wooden peg (rhymes with towel).
4. Not messy.
6. Part of a boat that catches the wind.
7. Big empty spaces in the ground.
8. Catch an animal.
9. The detective solved the _ _ _ _.
10. Not fake.

Fit these animal names into the puzzle. We've filled in one word to get you started.

3 letters
ANT
APE
CAT
DOG

4 letters
BEAR
GOAT
LION
PUMA

5 letters
BISON
GOOSE
OTTER
TIGER
ZEBRA

6 letters
MARMOT
OCELOT

8 letters
ANTELOPE
BULLFROG
ELEPHANT

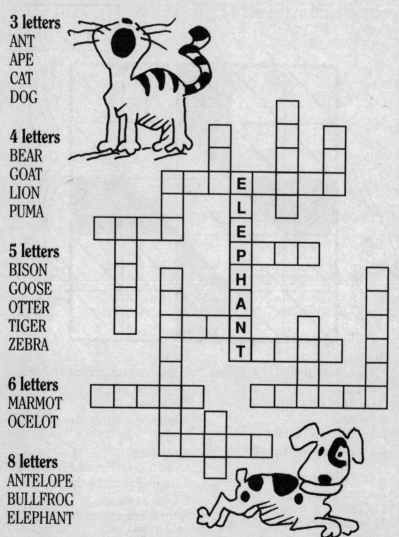

Unscramble these outer-space words.

1. EANIL (creature from another planet) __ __ __ __ __

2. SRTA (the sun is one of these) __ __ __ __

3. SRMA (name of a planet) __ __ __ __

4. KERTOC (spaceship) __ __ __ __ __ __

5. ORLAS (of or from the sun) __ __ __ __ __

6. NARSTU (name of a planet) __ __ __ __ __ __

7. LASTTILEE (manmade object that orbits the Earth)

__ __ __ __ __ __ __ __ __

8. AXLYAG (the Milky Way is one of these)

__ __ __ __ __ __

9. RUNAL (of or from the moon) __ __ __ __ __

10. UTLOP (name of a planet) __ __ __ __ __

Find the names of eleven animals hidden in this puzzle.
Start on the top line and read from left to right.

CAMELE
PHANTE
ATEREI
NDEERD
OGORIL
LAMALI
ONEWTI
GERBIL

Fit these baseball words into the puzzle. We've filled in one word to get you started.

3 letters
HIT
OUT

4 letters
BUNT
SAFE

5 letters
GLOVE
PLATE
SCORE
STEAL

6 letters
BATTER
INNING
SINGLE
STRIKE
TRIPLE

7 letters
CATCHER
PITCHER

8 letters
BASEBALL

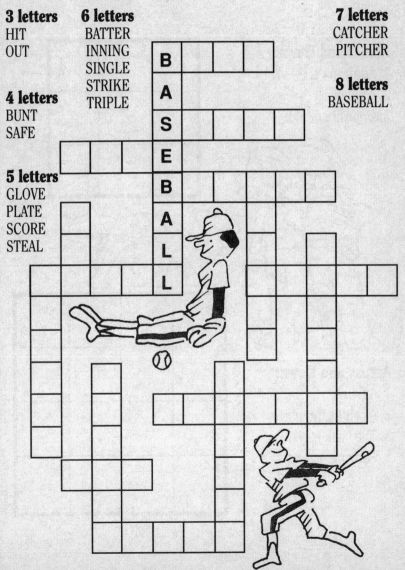

14 • Mini Crosswords

The answer for each numbered question is the same both across and down!

Across and Down:
1. Adult male.
2. A gorilla.
3. Opposite of old.

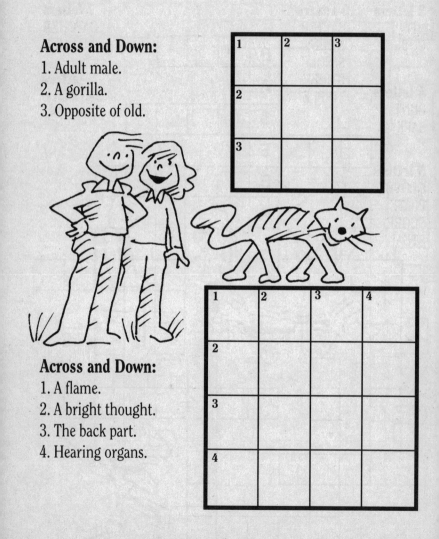

Across and Down:
1. A flame.
2. A bright thought.
3. The back part.
4. Hearing organs.

Spell each sports word by adding only one line to each letter (except letter "I").

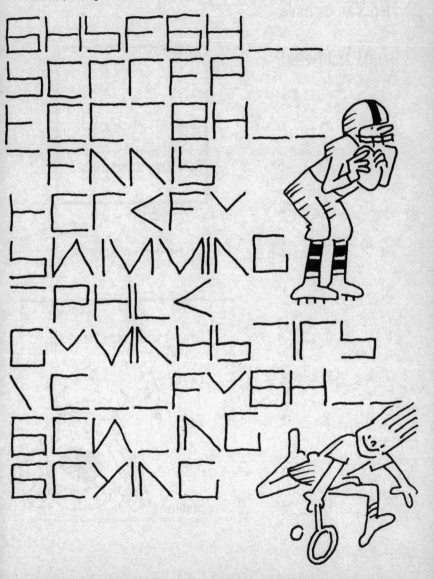

Each of these five-letter words has a vowel as its first, third, and fifth letters. Each missing letter is a consonant! Here's an example:

A W A R E   **Alert.**

1. E ___ A ___ E   Clean the blackboard.

2. E ___ O ___ E   Run away to marry.

3. U ___ I ___ E   Join together.

4. O ___ I ___ E   Oil used in cooking.

5. A ___ U ___ E   Entertain.

6. O ___ E ___ A   Drama with lots of singing.

7. A ___ I ___ E   Get up.

8. O ___ E ___ E   Fat.

9. I ___ A ___ E   Angry.

10. A ___ E ___ A   Stadium.

Do this puzzle like a regular crossword. But instead of filling in squares, put one letter in each triangle. For example, fill in the word FISH like this:

Across
1. A superhero sometimes wears a flowing _ _ _ _ (rhymes with tape).
3. Rip.
5. Close by.
6. Places where cows, chickens, or sheep often live.
7. Little _ _ _ _ Muffet.
8. A cord for a dog.
9. A tree with needles.
11. Picnic insects.
12. A very annoying person.

Down
1. A walking stick.
2. "A partridge in a _ _ _ _ tree."
3. When people cry, their eyes fill with _ _ _ _ _.
4. Two body limbs.
6. Trout, tuna, and salmon are different kinds of _ _ _ _.
7. Tall poles on ships.
8. To rest against something.
9. A Native American peace _ _ _ _.
10. A bird's home.

18 • Watermelon Word Game

Can you find at least eight 2-, 3-, 4-, and 5-letter words in the word WATERMELON? We've provided one of each to get you started.

TWO LETTERS	THREE LETTERS	FOUR LETTERS	FIVE LETTERS
AT	ATE	WEAR	WATER

Turn the top word into the bottom word by changing only one letter as you go down each step. You must change a different letter to form a new word at each step, until you have changed all four letters! (Hint: The last word in each puzzle shows you which new letters you must use as you go down each puzzle.) We've filled in one to give an example.

W	A	L	L
F	A	L	L
F	I	L	L
F	I	L	E
F	I	R	E

L I M B

___ ___ ___ ___

___ ___ ___ ___

___ ___ ___ ___

T A P E

B	A	R	N

___ ___ ___ ___

___ ___ ___ ___

C O N E

C O R N

___ ___ ___ ___

___ ___ ___ ___

___ ___ ___ ___

T I L E

1. Cross out the letters in the word CATS. Unscramble the remaining letters and spell the name of a fruit.

P	C	P
A	T	A
E	L	S

2. Cross out the letters in the word TREES. Unscramble the remaining letters and spell the name of a fruit.

E	R	A
E	T	E
R	S	P

3. Cross out the letters in the word DOG. Unscramble the remaining letters and spell the name of a fruit.

A	G	R
E	O	D
G	O	N

Change only one letter
in each word to
spell ten words
associated with horses.

1. BLINKERS   _ _ _ _ _ _ _ _

2. TALL   _ _ _ _

3. MAZE   _ _ _ _

4. ROOF   _ _ _ _

5. WALLOP   _ _ _ _ _ _

6. STALE   _ _ _ _ _

7. SHOW   _ _ _ _

8. TROD   _ _ _ _

9. RAIN   _ _ _ _

10. PADDLE   _ _ _ _ _ _

Across

1. Bottom edge of a dress.
4. Corned-beef H _ _ _.
6. Tool to dig with.
9. My _ _ _ _ is John.
10. Sums up.
12. United States of _ _ _ _ _ _ _.
14. Hansel and _ _ _ _ _ _.
16. Abbreviation for Los Angeles.
17. Get up.
18. Opposite of no.
20. Bees' home.
23. Abbreviation for Pennsylvania.
24. Adhesive _ _ _ _ (rhymes with cape).

Down

1. The place you live in.
2. Another word for pine tree.
3. "Give _ _ liberty or give me death."
5. Opposite of hers.
6. Tiny creature that lives in a shell.
7. Meat that comes from a pig.
8. Your SHOE _ _ _ _ _ are untied!
11. Fruit from a certain kind of palm tree (rhymes with mate).
13. People of Ireland.
15. Sixth musical note.
18. Japanese money.
19. Salt and _ _ _PER.
20. "To _ _ or not to be."
21. He, she, or _ _.
22. Abbreviation for Virginia.

Unscramble these bird names.

GARDEN BIRDS:

LUEB YAJ _____

BROIN _____

ROWSPRA _____

LIOREO _____

ERWN _____

HUNTER BIRDS:

LOW _____

WAKH _____

OCLAFN _____

DRONOC _____

PYESOR _____

EATING BIRDS:

KYUTRE _____

NICHKEC _____

CKUD _____

OSEOG _____

ASTANHPE _____

WATER BIRDS:

ULGL _____

RENOH _____

ANPILEC _____

TROSK _____

WANS _____

24 • Football Kriss Kross

Fit these football words into the puzzle. We've filled in one word to get you started.

3 letters
END
HIT
REF

4 letters
BOOT
HALF
KICK
PASS

6 letters
CLEATS
HELMET
HUDDLE
TACKLE

7 letters
OFFSIDE

8 letters
FOOTBALL
FULLBACK
HALFBACK

9 letters
GOAL POSTS
INTERCEPT
TOUCHDOWN

F O O T B A L L

Circle the names of the following water animals in the puzzle. Look across, up and down, and diagonally.

BASS   COD   CRAB   EEL   FLOUNDER
FROG   JELLYFISH   MARLIN   OCTOPUS   PERCH
SHARK   SHRIMP   TROUT   TUNA   WHALE

```
J X S Z A B C O D
E S H A R K F Y Z
L F R U E E L X S
L R I V I S O T A
Y O M Z S T U N A
F G P A B O N P M
I C B W R M D E A
S W R T H F E R R
H M R A T A R C L
R O O T B Z L H I
O C T O P U S E N
```

Can you find at least 25 words in the word RAINFALL?
(Don't forget to include one-letter words!)

_____   _____   _____

_____   _____   _____

_____   _____   _____

_____   _____   _____

_____   _____   _____

_____   _____   _____

_____   _____   _____

_____   _____   _____

How many lines must be drawn to connect each letter of the word TOUCAN to all the other letters?

28 • Scrambled Holidays

Unscramble the names of the ten holidays. Then print the circled letters, in order, in the spaces below to discover the name of a spring holiday.

1. ISTRMSHCA   _ _ _ _ _ _ ◯ _

2. OBRLA   _ _ ◯ _ DAY

3. NGVHITAGKSNI ◯_ _ _ _ _ _ _ _ _ _ _

4. UAKHNKHA ◯_ _ _ _ _ _ _

5. OMLAIRME   _ ◯ _ _ _ _ _ _ DAY

6. ETRESA   _ _ _ _ ◯ _

7. SUMBCLOU   _ _ _ _ _ _ _◯DAY

8. PNEDENIECNED _ _◯_ _ _ _ _ _ _ _ _ DAY

9. NELOAHELW   _◯_ _ _ _ _ _ _

10. WNE ASYRE   _ _ _ _ ◯_ _ _ ' DAY

SPRING HOLIDAY:

_ _ _ _ _ _ _ _ ' _   _ _ _

As you go down a step in each puzzle, subtract one letter to form a new word. Each step has a clue to help you.

1. **PAINT**

2. _ _ _ _ _   Hurt feeling.

3. _ _ _ _   Frying _ _ _ .

4. _ _   Adult male: M _ _ .

5. _   First letter.

1. **CROWN**

2. _ _ _ _ _   Black bird.

3. _ _ _ _   Farm animal.

4. _ _   Hurt sound.

5. _   Fifteenth letter.

The answer for each numbered question is the same both across and down.

Across and Down:
1. Beautiful, white lake bird.
2. Thin, strong metal strand.
3. Things shaped like curves or half circles (rhymes with parks).
4. Bird's home.

Across and Down:
1. Where's there's smoke, there's _ _ _ _.
2. A strong metal.
3. A path for cars.
4. The last pieces (rhymes with bends).

Across and Down:
1. Superhero's cloak.
2. When telephoning long distance, dial the _ _ _ _ code first.
3. Annoying person.
4. Dines.

Change only one letter in each word to spell seven words associated with:

TREES

1. LEAP _____
2. BANK _____
3. LAMB _____
4. RIOT _____
5. FEED _____
6. SCORN _____
7. TWIN _____

HOUSES

1. WINNOW _____
2. POOR _____
3. MATH _____
4. FALL _____
5. FLOOD _____
6. ZOOM _____
7. WOOF _____

Circle all the "sporty" words in the puzzle. Look across, up and down, and diagonally.

BASEBALL	BIKER	BOWLING	BOXER	CHESS
DARTS	FOOTBALL	HOCKEY	RACE	SAILING
SKIER	SOCCER	SWIM	TENNIS	

```
F X C D A R T S T
S O Y H W F M T E
W B O X E R Z B N
I O S T O S Y I N
M W A O B P S K I
Z L I R C A J E S
S I L A T C L R K
K N I C I L E L O
I G N E M X Z R V
E V G H O C K E Y
R B A S E B A L L
```

Find the names of nine birds hidden in this puzzle.
Start on the top line (but not necessarily the first letter)
and read from left to right.

Across

1. Bird that sometimes sounds like a cat.
5. Abbreviation for United States of America.
7. Either _ _.
8. Superheroes: _ _ _ _ _ _ and Robin.
10. Mammal that loves to play in water.
11. Opposite of lose.
13. Large body of fresh water: _ _ K E.
14. Backbone: S _ _ _ _.
15. Young adult (rhymes with mean).
17. Upon.
18. To change or make different (rhymes with Walter).
19. Seven days in a _ _ _ K.
21. Golf-ball peg.
22. Little Orphan _ _ _ _ _.
23. Beam of light.

Down

1. Cowboys tend them (rhymes with rattle).
2. Rip.
3. Legendary outlaw: _ _ _ _ _ Hood.
4. Abbreviation for doctor.
5. German submarine.
6. Past tense of sit.
9. Nasty.
11. Snowy season.
12. Almost.
14. A flag flies on it.
16. Level.
18. Dined.
19. Abbreviation for Western Australia.
20. Write with a P _ _.

A word is spelled in the shaded diagonal squares of each block. Change the word in the shaded squares by switching the order of the across words in each block. Here's an example:

Change WAR to FIR.

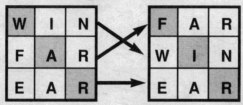

Now try these:

Change PINK to TIRE.

P	A	N	E
F	I	R	E
P	I	N	T
T	A	N	K

T			
	I		
		R	
			E

Change NOBLE to ROBOT.

N	O	I	S	E
C	O	L	O	R
H	A	B	I	T
T	A	B	L	E
R	A	N	G	E

R				
	O			
		B		
			O	
				T

36 • Scrambled Trees

Unscramble the names of these trees. Then print the circled letters, in order, in the spaces below to discover the name of a beautiful Australian tree.

1. CHEEB ___ ◯ ___ ___ ___
2. TNUWLA ___ ___ ___ ___ ___ ◯ ___
3. RIBHC ___ ___ ___ ◯ ___
4. LAMP ___ ◯ ___ ___
5. MEL ___ ◯ ___
6. KIHCROY ___ ___ ___ ___ ___ ___ ◯
7. PLEMA ___ ___ ◯ ___ ___
8. CTESHTUN ___ ___ ___ ___ ◯ ___ ___ ___
9. PULIT ___ ◯ ___ ___ ___
10. CRUEPS ◯ ___ ___ ___ ___ ___

Australian tree:

___ ___ ___ ___ ___ ___ ___ ___ ___

Find the names of eight flowers hidden in this puzzle.
Start on the top line (but not necessarily the first letter)
and read from left to right.

ADAHLI
ASTERO
SEIRIS
MARIGO
LDENRO
DAFFOD
ILILAC

38 • Change-a-Word

Change each of these words into another word by simply changing the order of the letters. Here's an example:

PEA	____	BASTE	_____
ATE	____ or ____	SNAKE	_____
NOT	____	BOARD	_____
WON	____ or ____	NORSE	_____
TEN	____	COULD	_____
SUE	____	SHALE	_____
LEFT	_____	WARDEN	_____
LILT	_____	SILVER	_____
ONCE	_____	DANGER	_____
NEWT	_____	DAGGER	_____
ODOR	_____	RESIST	_____
TERN	_____	BAWLER	_____

Circle the names of the school subjects in the puzzle. Look across, up and down, and diagonally.

ARITHMETIC   ART   ENGLISH   GEOGRAPHY
GYM   HEALTH   HISTORY   MUSIC
READING   SCIENCE   WRITING

```
S W R I T I N G A
Y C X M C L M R R
G Z I I F Y R E I
L E S E G Q L A T
L U O N N Z Y D H
M H P G B C T I M
R E S L R N E N E
T A N I D A E G T
A L V S W Z P Q I
R T V H O X T H C
T H H I S T O R Y
```

How many lines must be drawn to connect each letter of the word MOOSE to all the other letters?

Do this puzzle like a regular crossword. But instead of filling in squares, put one letter in each triangle. For example, fill in the word FISH like this:

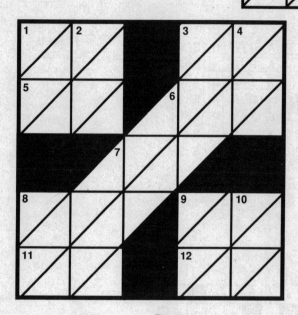

Across
1. Little, tunnel-digging animal.
3. Dark-colored soft drink.
5. Gather a crop.
6. Big machine that lifts heavy objects.
7. The quarterback threw the _ _ _ _.
8. A clam lives in one.
9. The cook will _ _ _ _ a cake.
11. Dines.
12. "House for _ _ _ _."

Down
1. Many, _ _ _ _, most.
2. Jump.
3. Tiny skeletons that make up a reef (rhymes with moral).
4. Narrow little street or path.
6. To telephone someone.
7. These hold up pants.
8. Name of baseball's New York Mets' stadium (rhymes with may).
9. To ride a horse without a saddle: _ _ _ _BACK.
10. Clark _ _ _ _ (Superman).

page 4:

GIRAFFE, ELK, PUMA, OWL, MOLE,
TURKEY, RABBIT, ROOSTER

page 5:

page 6:

page 7:

1. BLAME
2. LAME
3. LAM
4. LA
5. A

1. PLANET
2. PLANE
3. PLAN
4. PAN
5. PA
6. P

1. FINGER
2. FINER
3. FINE
4. FIN
5. IN
6. I

page 8:

1. ISLAND
2. FISH
3. VISE
4. OASIS
5. SISTER
6. MISSISSIPPI
7. KISS
8. PROMISE
9. MIST
10. MISTER

page 9:

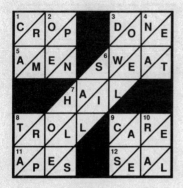

page 11:

1. ALIEN
2. STAR
3. MARS
4. ROCKET
5. SOLAR
6. SATURN
7. SATELLITE
8. GALAXY
9. LUNAR
10. PLUTO

page 12:

CAMEL, ELEPHANT, ANTEATER, REIN-
DEER, DOG, GORILLA, LLAMA, LION,
NEWT, TIGER, GERBIL

page 10:

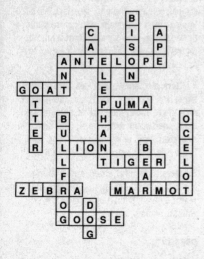

page 13:

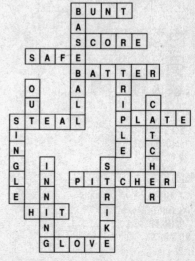

page 14:

1 M	2 A	3 N
2 A	P	E
3 N	E	W

1 F	2 I	3 R	4 E
2 I	D	E	A
3 R	E	A	R
4 E	A	R	S

page 15:

BASEBALL
SOCCER
FOOTBALL
TENNIS
HOCKEY
SWIMMING
TRACK
GYMNASTICS
VOLLEYBALL
BOWLING
BOXING

page 16:

1. ERASE
2. ELOPE
3. UNITE
4. OLIVE
5. AMUSE
6. OPERA
7. ARISE
8. OBESE
9. IRATE
10. ARENA

page 17:

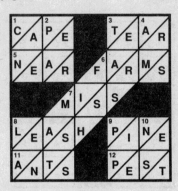

page 18:

2 letters: am, an, me, no, on, or, to, we.

3 letters: ant, are, arm, art, awe, awn, ear, eat, eel, eon, era, ere, ewe, lam, law, lea, let, lot, low, man, mat, men, nee, net, new, nor, now, oar, oat, one, ore, owe, own, ram, ran, rat, raw, rot, row, tan, tar, ten, toe, ton, tow, wan, war, wee, won.

4 letters: alee, anew, ante, earl, earn, elan, lame, late, lean, lent, lore, mart, mean, meet, melt, mere, moat, molt, name, near, neat, newt, noel, norm, note, omen, oral, rant, rate, ream, reel, rete, team, tern, tone, tore, tram, tree, want, warm, wart, welt, wren.

5 letters: alert, alter, eaten, enter, later, learn, lemon, melon, metro, moral, orate, realm, Roman, talon, tenor, towel, tower, woman, women, wrote.

page 19:

BARN	or	BARN	or	BARN		
BORN		BORN		BARE		
CORN		BORE		CARE		
CORE		CORE		CORE	or	CANE
CONE		CONE		CONE		

page 19 (continued):

LIMB	or LIMB	or LIMB	CORN
LIME	LAMB	LIME	TORN
TIME	LAME	LAME	TORE
TAME	TAME	TAME	TIRE
TAPE	TAPE	TAPE	TILE

page 20:

1. APPLE
2. PEAR
3. ORANGE

page 21:

1. BLINDERS
2. TAIL
3. MANE or MARE
4. HOOF
5. GALLOP

6. STALL
7. SHOE
8. TROT
9. REIN
10. SADDLE

page 22:

page 23:

Garden Birds:	Hunter Birds:
blue jay	owl
robin	hawk
sparrow	falcon
oriole	condor
wren	osprey

page 23 (continued):

Eating Birds:	Water Birds:
turkey	gull
chicken	heron
duck	pelican
goose	stork
pheasant	swan

page 24:

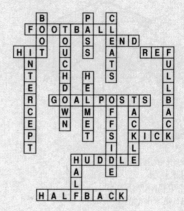

page 25:

page 26:

a, an, ail, air, all, far, fan, fin, fir, fall, fail, fair, fill, frill, flair, flail, frail, final, I, if, in, ill, nail, la, lain, lair, liar, ran, rail, rain, rill.

page 27:

Fifteen lines are needed.

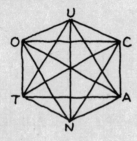

page 28:

1. CHRISTMAS
2. LABOR
3. THANKSGIVING
4. HANUKKAH
5. MEMORIAL
6. EASTER
7. COLUMBUS
8. INDEPENDENCE
9. HALLOWEEN
10. NEW YEAR'S

Spring Holiday: MOTHER'S DAY

page 29:

1. PAINT	1. CROWN
2. PAIN	2. CROW
3. PAN	3. COW
4. AN	4. OW
5. A	5. O

page 30:

¹S	²W	³A	⁴N
²W	I	R	E
³A	R	C	S
⁴N	E	S	T

¹F	²I	³R	⁴E
²I	R	O	N
³R	O	A	D
⁴E	N	D	S

¹C	²A	³P	⁴E
²A	R	E	A
³P	E	S	T
⁴E	A	T	S

page 31:

Tree words:
1. LEAF
2. BARK
3. LIMB
4. ROOT
5. SEED
6. ACORN
7. TWIG

House words:
1. WINDOW
2. DOOR
3. BATH
4. WALL
5. FLOOR
6. ROOM
7. ROOF

page 32:

page 33:

REDWING, GRACKLE, EGRET, THRUSH, CANARY, CROW, OWL, LARK, KESTREL

page 34:

page 35:

Change PINK to TIRE:

Change NOBLE to ROBOT:

page 36:

1. BEECH
2. WALNUT
3. BIRCH
4. PALM
5. ELM
6. HICKORY
7. MAPLE
8. CHESTNUT
9. TULIP
10. SPRUCE

Australian tree: **EUCALYPTUS**

page 37:

DAHLIA, ASTER, ROSE, IRIS, MARIGOLD, GOLDENROD, DAFFODIL, LILAC

page 38:

1. PEA	APE
2. ATE	TEA or EAT
3. NOT	TON
4. WON	OWN or NOW
5. TEN	NET
6. SUE	USE

1. LEFT	FELT
2. LILT	TILL
3. ONCE	CONE
4. NEWT	WENT
5. ODOR	DOOR
6. TERN	RENT

48 • Answers

page 38 (continued):
page 41:

1. BASTE	BEAST
2. SNAKE	SNEAK
3. BOARD	BROAD
4. NORSE	SNORE
5. COULD	CLOUD
6. SHALE	LEASH

1. WARDEN	WANDER
2. SILVER	SLIVER or LIVERS
3. DANGER	GARDEN or GANDER
4. DAGGER	RAGGED
5. RESIST	SISTER
6. BAWLER	WARBLE

page 39:

```
S W R I T I N G A
Y C X M C L M R R
G Z I I F Y R E I
L E S E G Q L A T
U O N N Z Y D I H
M H P G B C T N M
R E S L R N E G E
T A N I D A E   T
A L V S W Z P Q I
R T V H O X T H C
T H H I S T O R Y
```

page 40:

Ten lines are needed.

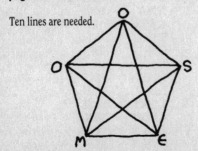